Zodiac Publishing Services

Presents

A Simple Guide to Software Testing!

Life Grows With Us!

Manual & Automation Testing!

By
G. R. Narasimhan

Testing Extends to Prototype!

Zodiac Services, Chennai, India

Get more contact details and numbers from:

www.zodiacservices.org [or] mail to info@zodiacservices.org

Ordering Information for hardcopies:

Quantity sales - Special discounts are available on quantity purchases by corporations, associations, and others. For details, contact the author at the address above.

JUNE 2023 – First Edition

Released and Published from India.

ABOUT THE AUTHOR

G.R. Narasimhan – Engineer, Senior Technology Expert and Writer; having interest/hobby to serve the mankind in alternative beliefs astrological predictions, prayers, remedies, prasnam, vedic guidance for short or long term problems, vastu, numerology, gem stones, yantras, mantras or rituals (related areas), yoga, meditation, counselling, alternative therapies consulting. Business & education, soft skills training & promotion, web designing, career counselling and internet & social media marketing additionally. Assisting for the above mentioned areas to serve better, he is also the author of few eBooks called "A Simple guide to Vedic Astrology", "Symbolic Meditation"/ "Third Eye Astrology", "MBA Basics in 24 Hrs", "Vastu Architecture and Feng Shui Science", "Numerology and Baby Names", "Maths power Made easy", "A Small Green Book – LOA" etc (are available in Amazon) having extended experience in IT + Management areas developed the website and online marketing using different business strategies and continue the service very well to extend further including this "A Simple Guide to Software Testing" – in the technology books series; specifically based on the real time experience and scenarios from technology trend and growth. With the continuous extraordinary ability and skills in research and experience, he is able to explain and train/ assist others with extended support and guidance by counselling/ consulting effectively. Also many devotional books like Hanuman, Narayana, Varahi, Gayatri, Shiva, Durga, Navagraha Upasana/worship books are available from zodiac services in Amazon!

Great thanks and good luck for everyone whoever reading this book on "A Simple Guide to Software Testing" with your extreme ideas and willingness to enhance your knowledge and power to be a best technology/quality expert. Wishing you good luck to be in the zone of healthy learning! For any queries and feedback, you can contact directly via email to: info@zodiacservices.org or astronara@gmail.com

Contents

Chapters	Page #
Introduction	5
Software Testing Introduction and Types	6
Testing Categories	6
Software Development Life Cycle	7
Software Development Model	9
Testing Levels	11
Test Plan Preparation	12
Detailed Test Cases	14
Test Execution	16
Test Problem (Fault) Report (TPR)	18
Special Testing Methods	20
Requirements Traceability Matrix (RTM)	23
Defect Analysis	24
Test Strategy Preparation (Master Test Plan)	25
Test Automation	28
Sample Testing tools for Automation	29
Agile & DevOps Testing	30
Test Management Tools	31
Summary & Conclusion	32

Note: Some of the areas are covered with our own advertisements in this book. They are not any ousider or company ads; but our own Zodiac Publishing books only. If required, you can search those books in Amazon and make use of them. Sorry for the inconvenience and thanks for your cooperation!

Introduction

Welcome to the world of software testing, where the effectiveness and reliability of software applications are put to the ultimate test. In this book, "Manual and Automated Software Testing," we embark on a journey to explore the intricate realm of software testing, shedding light on both manual and automated techniques that play a vital role in ensuring software quality in brief and simple way.

In today's digital age, where software applications have become an integral part of our daily lives, it is essential to deliver products that not only meet user expectations but also function flawlessly. Software testing serves as the cornerstone of this process, enabling organizations to identify defects, mitigate risks, and provide a seamless user experience.

You can learn the fundamentals & types of Software Testing, the key concepts, methodologies, and terminologies that form the basis of this discipline. From test planning and test case design to test execution and defect management, we cover the entire testing life cycle, providing you with a solid foundation.

We delve into the world of manual testing, where human intervention plays a crucial role. We explore various techniques such as black-box testing, white-box testing, and grey-box testing, explaining their purpose and how they are executed. Through practical examples and real-world scenarios, we demonstrate how manual testing can effectively uncover defects and validate software functionality.

Software Quality Automation has revolutionized the field of software testing, enabling faster and more efficient validation of applications. In this chapter, we demystify test automation, shedding light on the tools, frameworks, and best practices involved.

Combining Manual and Automated Testing for Optimal Results While manual and automated testing techniques each have their strengths, combining them strategically can yield remarkable results. We also explore how manual and automated testing can complement each other, creating a robust testing approach.

Effective test management and documentation are critical to any successful testing endeavor. We explore test management tools and methodologies that help streamline the testing process and ensure clear communication between testers, developers, and stakeholders.

Special Testing area, software applications must also meet performance and security standards. The performance testing and security testing, two specialized areas within software testing. We discuss testing methods to evaluate application performance under different conditions and methods to identify vulnerabilities and protect against potential threats.

We can also explore emerging trends such as artificial intelligence, machine learning, and DevOps, and their impact on the testing landscape. We also discuss the importance of continuous testing in an agile development environment. More advanced topics could be found from various online resources. Wish you good luck!

Software Testing

Software testing is the process of evaluating and verifying that a software product or application that what it has to do including the behavior of the software by validation and verification. The main aim of testing is to maintain the quality of the product developed fully or partially. Software testing can also provide an objective, independent view of the software to allow the business to appreciate & understand the risks of software implementation.Also, identifies any issues and defects with the written code so they can be fixed before the software product is delivered. Improves product quality. When it comes to customer area, delivering a quality product is an important metric to consider.

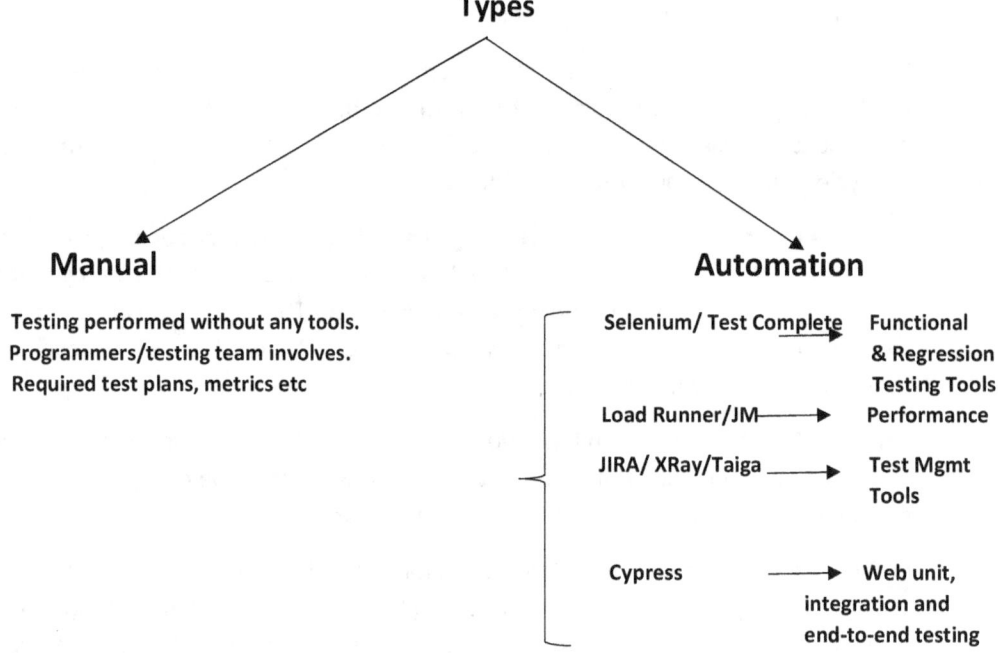

Testing Categories

WBT (White Box Testing)
- Done by developer (or Programmer).
- Line by Line testing performed.
- i/p, o/p, programs and database are tested.

BBT (Black Box Testing)
- Functional testing done.
- All the files/modules/pages are tested.
- .EXE Files, Web pages, APIs, etc (quality and customer satisfaction).
- Testing team involves.

GBT (Gray Box Testing)
- Combination of WBT and BBT.
- Only in few companies, they do follow both individually. Agile/DevOps as well.

SDLC (Software Development Life Cycle)

The software development life cycle completely involves from the inception to maintenance activities. Applicable for agiles/devops methodologies as well.

I)   INCEPTION
The following are stages/steps to be considered in the inception phase.
1. Request for Proposal - Tender
2. Proposal   - Cost, Technology, S/W & H/W Standard, No. of People, Credential.
3. Negotiation   - Selecting a company from many (who are proposed).
4. Letter of Intend (LOI) & discussion
5. Contract signed   ⟶   P.M. (from Client)
                                          P.M. (from Company)

II)   Requirement Specification
Specific requirements are collected for the users and software/technology by the analysts.
1. U.R.S -   User Requirement Specification (User Language)
2. S.R.S   - Software/System Requirement Specification
    -   (B.A)   or   (S.A)
    - Business Analyst   System Analyst
    - Functional (flow of modules/methods)
    - FSD (Functional Signature Domain)

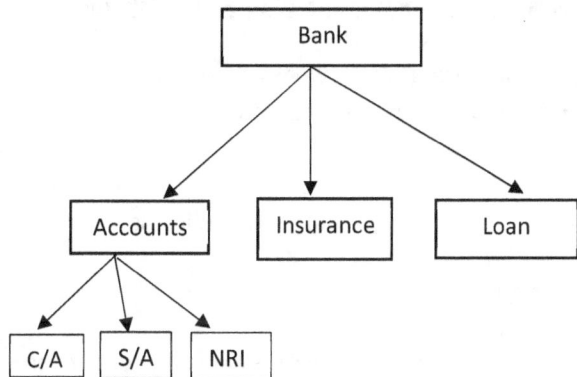

III)   Designing:
1. **HLD**
    High Level Design   (i) Top Down
    (i)   Done by B.A. or S.A.
    (ii)   Two Approaches <
                                                    (ii) Bottom Up

Top down approach involves splitting the whole high level requirements or operations in to different sub modules or tasks. Bottom up design goes from smaller tasks or modules to give a big picture of the whole design.

2. LLD

Low Level Design

- Screen (forms), buttons,outer objects.
- In the depth designing in the HLD.

IV) **Coding** ⟶ Done by Developers using LLD (Low Level Design) with appropriate technology, front end, backend and database etc.

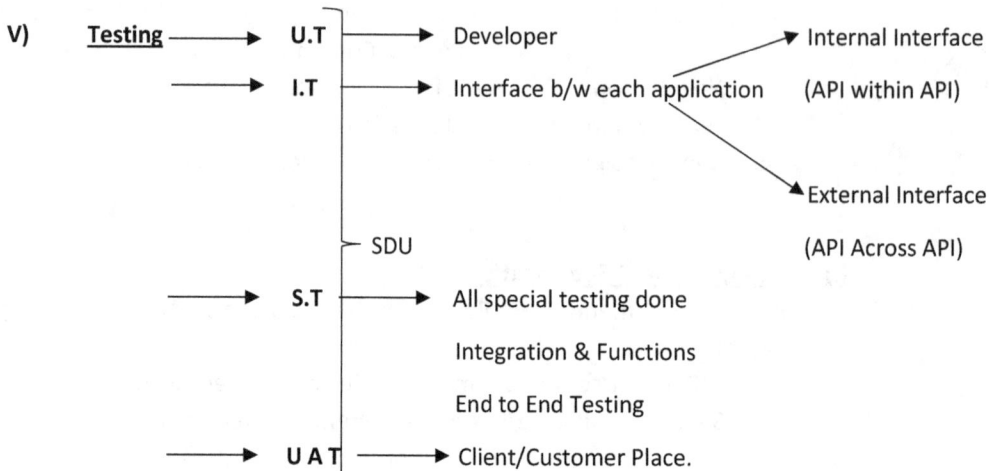

Unit Testing, Integration Testing, System Testing and User Acceptance Testing are done.

VI) **Releasing the products and 30 to 90 days Warranty Period**

Some companies are giving 2 weeks to 90 days post live support and warranty for any fixes or changes as per the requirements.

(i)   30 to 90 days no pay.
(ii)   After 90 days charge as applicable.

VII) **Maintanence:**

In the maintenance phase, it covers issue fixing, enhancement, customer support etc.

(i)   Bug Fixing   ⟶   Testing and Development.
(ii)   Enhancement   ⟶   Testing and Development.
(iii)   Upgradation   ⟶   Version(newer)   1.0,1.1 etc;

Software Development Models

(1) Water fall Model

Example:

In the Banking project example if you consider 3 Months timeline, then check the flow of each phase below.

(Project Time)

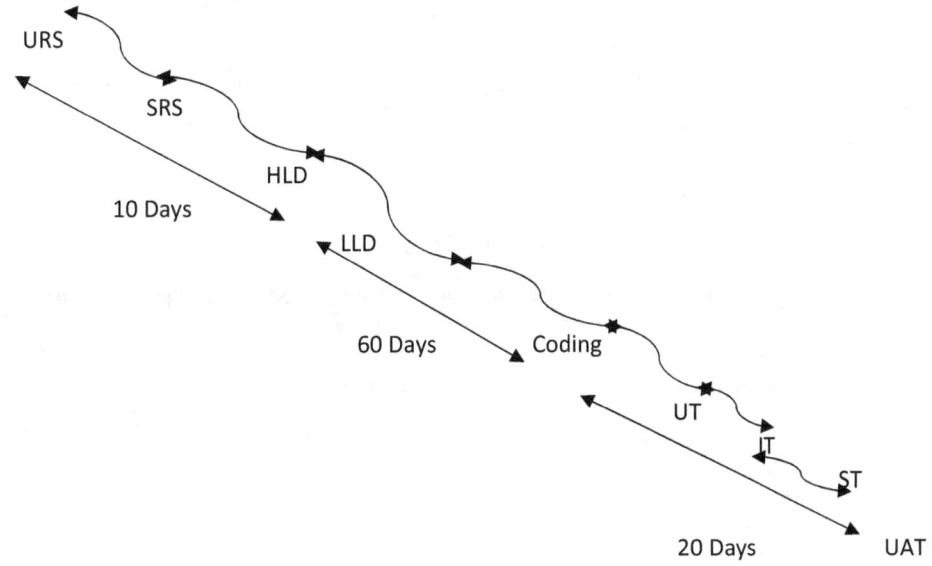

(2) Spiral (or) Incremental Model:

In the Spiral model, similar to waterfall model; it goes in the incremental way.
But, on the need basis, it works like agile.

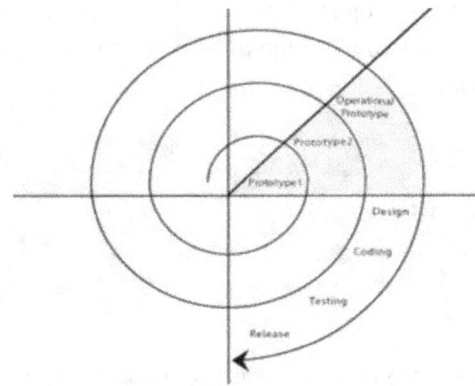

(3) Extreme Program Model:

- After One Module -> Testing Starts immediately like agile.
- Documentation - Preparation will differ from Spiral.

(4) Prototype Model:

- Limited Working Model.
- Based on the Sample, original developed and implemented to client/customer.

(5) Vee Model: -> Most Popular Model in MNCs. Unit test conducted for coding, Integrated testing done for designed modules functions, System Testing done for System/Software requirements and then UAT for user requirements.

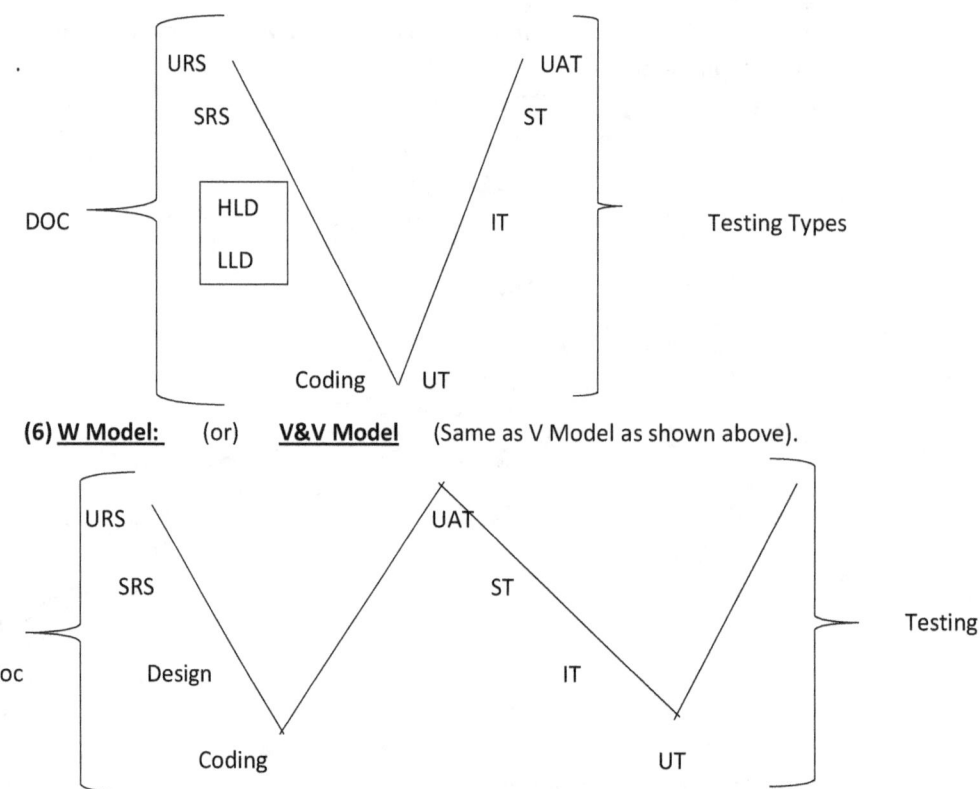

(6) W Model: (or) **V&V Model** (Same as V Model as shown above).

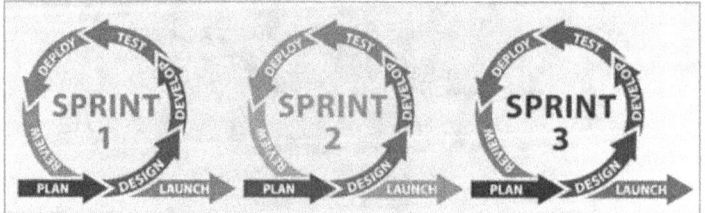

(7) Agile Model

Agile approach divides project(s) into smaller iterations or sections handled in sprints (2 weeks timelines). The scope & requirements of the project are defined at the start of the development phase.

(8) DevOps Model

Combination of software development (Dev) and operations (Ops). A software engineering methodology which aims to integrate the work of development teams & operations teams by facilitating a culture of collaboration & shared responsibility.

Testing Levels

(1) UTL (Unit Test Level)

→ Developer/tool Checks the coding
→ Line by Line Check happens
→ Syntax and Logical Errors are covered
→ I/p and o/p data are tested
→ Programs as well as associated data to be tested

(2) ITL (Integration Testing Level)

● Tester (or) Testing Team will test module. Sometimes development team itself will test.

(i)	Internal Interface	(ii)	External Interface
	Ex: ICICI/BOFA Server		Ex: (HDFC -> ICICI) between different banks
	(Between ICICI Bank Servers)		

(3) STL (System Test Levels)

Many special testing are also covered at this level. End to end testing to be completed before UAT.

→ End to End Testing
→ Functionality
→ Special Testing

● Load Volume Testing (under normal and high volumes of data tested)
● Stress Testing (Testing beyond the limits of normal operations)
● Scalability (Increasing no. of users testing - type of load testing)
● Interoperability testing (A software with other software or OS etc)
● Recovery Testing (Crashes and recovery of data etc)
● Usability Testing(Testing from the user's perspective)
● Bench Marking (Comparison of software products)
● Smoke Testing (Checking the software application to move next level)

(4) UATL (User Acceptance Test Level)

→ End user will test the developed and tested application and then gives go/no go for implementation. It has to fulfill all the user requirements.

*Note: -> Testing can be done only (2) and (3) stages as described above.
        -> All the other testing will be done in stage (2) including special testing.

Testing and Debugging Difference

Testing	Debugging
*Tester	*Developer
*Identify the Bugs	*Fix the Bugs
*.exe/cloud application etc	*Coding
* (Using Testing Tools)	*(By Programmer manually)

Test Plan Preparation

→ Prepared by Test Lead/Manager.
→ Prepared especially based on the ETVX criteria.

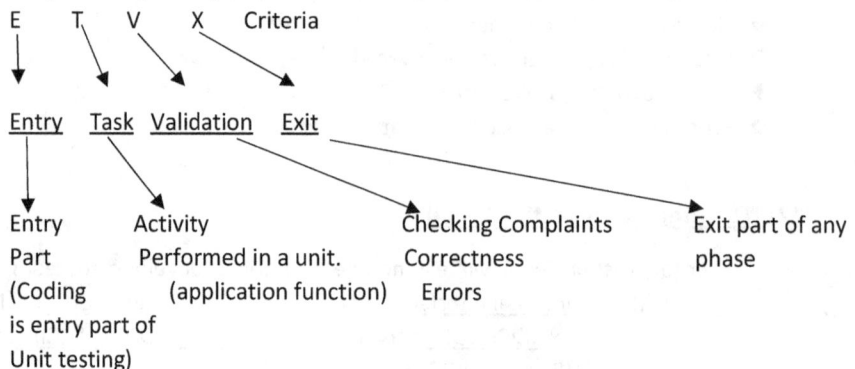

Based on this ETVX, many documents prepared at different stages of testing. Some are given in the following examples as what are the details to be captured in the documents.

I) **Unit Test (plan/doc)**

    1. What? i/p and o/p units. -> separate documents for input and output

    2. +ve Test case first or
        -ve Test case first   -> documents

    3. Sequence -> Checking order of plans

    4. Unit Test Matrix

       Matrix (functionality)

Fields	Valid/IP	Invalid/IP	Junk Input	Null I/P	Lower Char	Upper Char	Press
User ID	Sara	ABCDE	A*123	N/A	Min 4 Char	Max 16	N/A
Pwd	Sara	ABCDE	123*$	N/A	Min 4 Char	Max 16	N/A
OK							Yes
Cancel							Yes

II) Integration Test (plan/doc)

1. Internal Interface
2. External Interface
3. Sequence of Interfaces (Integration)

Integration Testing Definition/Execution	Input	Output	Expected Result	Actual Result	Invalid Data I/p	ID	Date/Time
Case 1							
Case 2							
...							

III) System Test (plan/doc)
(or) Detailed Test (doc)

1. Functionality
2. Configuration
3. Security
4. Performance
   - Preparing group (modules) doc.

IV) User Acceptance Test (plan/doc)

- Based on system Test Plan

Some Specific Test Plans

1) Unit Test Plan (Mostly covers..)

1. Unit testing tools.
2. Priority of Program Units.
3. Naming Conversion of test cases.
4. Status reporting mechanism.

2) Integration Test Plan: (Mostly covers...)

1. Priority of program interface.
2. Naming Conversion of all test cases.
3. Status reporting mechanism.
   Note: No specific test plans for STP and UATP.

* Above Unit and Integration test plans are used in most of the cases.

* QA & UAT environments are used to test before application is moving in to production.

Detailed Test Cases

- The proof of the testing and detailed document.

Template of Details Test Cases:

Test Case ID → Unique Identifier across the company/project.

Test Case Description → Brief description about the test.

Test pre-requisites → What the system should have while testing?

Test Inputs → Input data given as peer description → optional.

Test Steps → Step by step instructions based on description and inputs.

Expected Result → Expectation result of input description and inputs.

Actual result→ Present situation in the system (actual output).

Status (pass/ fail) → If match result then pass otherwise fail.

Note: This also follows matrix format of documentation.

Test Case Example (Student Registration Screen)

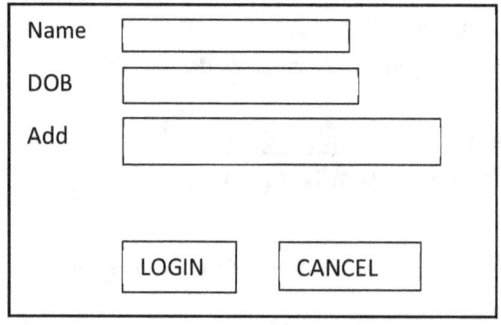

1) Functionality: To register and give number to a student.

- ve Test Case:

Test Case ID → Student, Reg-Screen 1

Test Case Description → To test system rejects invalid month.

Test Pre-requisites→ the user should have access to register through student Reg- Screen.

Test Inputs → **Name = "Nara"**

→DOB = 24/20/

Invalid

→ Address = **"13 Swami Street"**

Test Steps → Give value to the fields in the screen as per the test inputs.

2. Click Login Button

Expected Result → The system must say

"Month must be between 1 and 12

To check the value and

Resubmit"

Actual result → at the time of execution

(Output on screen)

Status → Actual Result is equal to Expected Result

+ve- Test Cases:

Test Case ID → Student Reg- Screen1

Test Case Description → System Accepts Valid Month

Test pre- requisition → User should have access to the register

Test inputs → Name = "Nara"

DOB = "24/02/75"

Address = "12 Abstract"

Test Steps → Give values to fields in the screen as per the Test inputs

Expected Result → The System must display message

"Thanks for registering. Your Roll No: is 12345"

→ The information is stored in STUDENT'S TABL- with roll number equals to

12345

Actual Result → At the time of execution.

Status → Actual Result is matched with Expected Result

Advertisement:

Test Execution

- Test Cases are prepared, collected and stored in a central location from where all team members can read and share the test case details.
- These test cases are reviewed by lead tester and approved by the same lead tester/Manager.
- The next action item is to executing test cases.
- So the program units that are to be tested using these test cases and to be ready.
- 1. Test Case Distribution.

2. Test Environment Setup. (Few changes might be followed for cloud based systems)

      (i) There must be no development tools installed in a test bed.

      (ii) Ensure the OS and Service pack installed.

      (iii) Ensure the disk have enough memory space.

      (iv) Carry out a virus check if needed.

      (v) Ensure the integrity of web server.

      (vi) Ensure the integrity of database server.

3. Test Data/Steps Preparation.

4. Actual Test Execution.

(i) **Install Test** (after getting .exe/project/application file).

- Download from cloud/repository and do (auto) install in default mode.[for system and mobile]. Then track the following.
- Does installer checks for prerequisites S/W to be installed?
- Does installer check for system user privileges?
- Does installer check for sufficient disk memory space?
- Does installer check for licence agreement?
- Does installer check for right product key?
- Does installer check on default path/ new path/ Non-Existence path?
- Do we have different installed type like custom, full, compact, typical etc. [lite or full]?
- Cancel installation halfway through.
- Uninstall the Software.
- Cancel installation halfway through un-install.
- Re-install on the same machine/mobile device.
- Repair an existing install on the same machine/mobile device.
- Does installer create folders, icons, Shortcut Keys, Files, Database tables, registry keys.
- Does (uninstall) (or) removes any other files do not belong to this product.

(ii) **Navigation Tests**

- Move to every possible screens using menus, tool bar items, shortcut keys (or) Links.
- Check for respective screen title and screen fields for the existence.
- Move back and front from various screens to other forms in ad-hoc manner.
- Exit the application and restart the application many times.

(iii) Build Verification Test (BVT):

Once the Navigation test completed, execute the test that are critical- that means, a set of test cases must be identified as is a critical priority such that, if then these test do not work, Product does not get acceptance from the test team. Usually this will be 10 to 15 % of total test cases.

Any add, insert possibilities automatically falls under BVT, because if we cannot add we will be blocked from modify/ delete/ view etc.

(iv) Build Acceptance Test (BAT):

Next job is to go through 90% of test cases in the respective test steps one by one and then actually performing steps on the software products. This involves feeding the values to the PGM as per the test input and then performing other actions in the sequence as given in the test steps. When the input are fed, the system is suppose to react according to the design. Whatever happen after the actions are performed on the system the tester will have to write the result in the actual result section after test cases.

* Ideally the expected result and the actual result must match, if the program is designed and indeed. When they match, the test cases treated as Pass or else Fail.

* The testing achieved its goals by identifying such failure in the software.

* After the actual results are recorded, the pass/fail criteria is determined by the individual testers, the test case sheets are reviewed and it is ensured that pass/ fail criteria is correctly determined. Sometimes because of inexperience, tester may think a failure as pass and Vice Versa. But the load tester must ultimately approved the pass/ fail criteria in the test cases.

Test Problem (Fault) Report (TPR)

Test Problem Reports (TPR) related to the deficiencies/issues found in the test results, and track problem(s) until they are completely resolved.

1. TPR ID -> Unique ID number across content.
2. TPR Description -> A brief description of the problem.
3. TPR Date -> The date on which the TPR is raised.
4. Author -> The tester who raise the TPR..
5. T.C. (Test Case) ID -> The Test Case that caused this TPR to be raised.
6. Software Version -> The Version number of software that was tested and found fault.
7. Problem Severity -> Changing field like High/ Medium/Low. This will be agreed by the   Lead Tester and the development Project Manager.
8. Problem Description -> The description of what was tested and what happened. This will be filled by the tester.
9. Problem Re-Solution -> after fixing the problem, the developer fills this section, with details about the fix (problem).
10. Assigned to -> to whom the TPR is assigned to be fixed (problem).
11. Expected Closure Date -> when the problem is to be closed.
12. Actual Closure Date -> when the problem is actually rectified and closed.
13. TPR Status -> This is the changing field to reflect the status of the TPR.
    * Ir-reproductive – Problem (unsolved or unable to reproduce). To solve this -> [Test Lead, development, Project Manager]
    Triage Meeting -> If development do not accept problem.

    (i)   Bug Life Cycle

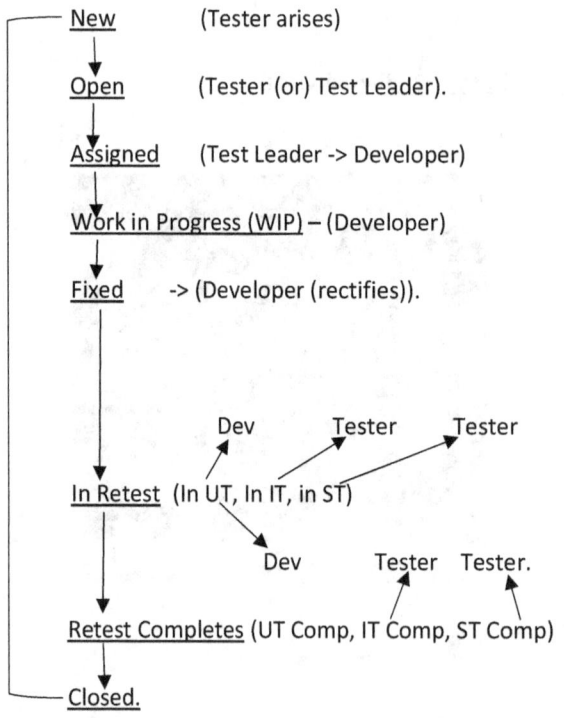

(ii) Test Records

(i)   Based on Test Case ID:

Test Case ID	Test Priority	Executed	Pass/Fail Y/N	TPR Number	Date of Last Execution	Responsibility

(ii)   Report Based on TPR:

TPR Number	TPR Severity	Test Case ID	TPR Author	TPR Status	TPR Date	Expected Closure Date	Actual Closure Date	Assigned to

- Individual testers/programmers will be sending their status on executing the test cases to the lead testers/QA lead, on a timely basis as described in the test Plan Documents.
- This will include what are the test cases that the testers had executed during that period, which all passed (or) failed and the TPR which are raised based on the failed test cases.
- When the lead tester gets this status from individual tester, this will consolidate all the details and will arrive various kind of reports. This will be used for tracking testing activities and to plan further.
- There are 2 major reports which helps the lead tester and project manager to know about the status and progress of testing phases, one is based on (i) Test Case ID (ii) TPR Number.

(i)   **Test Case Summary :** (given to following)
(i) Total Number of Test Cases.
(ii) Number of Test Cases Executed.
(iii) Number of Test Case Passed.
(iv) Number of Test Case Failed.

(ii)   **TPR Summary:** (given to following)
(i) No. of TPR Generated.
(ii) No. of TPR Opened.
(iii) No. of TPR in Progress.
(iv) No. of TPR Closed.

Special Testing Methods

(i) Load Volume Testing (performance testing)

- Performance of the system is tested in two modes (i) one way the system database is heavily populated with the huge number of records, so this is an exception that the database will grow in millions/ enormous of the application usage (ii) At the later date, the performance may be slow, due to heavy volume of records in the database. After populating to database tables, if we do a set of system cases, we will come to know whether the system works with same response time (or) not.

(ii) Stress Testing

- In many applications, programs are accessed by multiple clients. When it comes to internet application number of concurrent user may go up to several thousands or even millions. In such cases the application must be able to later simultaneous requests without crashing or showing down. In this way the system is tested by huge no. of simultaneous requisites.
- By doing stress testing, we will come to know whether there are any bottlenecks that slowdown the process when the number users access application simultaneously.

(iii) Interoperability Testing

- Many Application are designed and developed in such a way that they can operate in variety of platforms, for example an internet gaming applications may have to run in platforms like Linux, NT, UNIX etc;[including mobile apps with android and IOS]
- As the range of people playing is wide and all from different geographical locations and from different fields.
- Also the same product will be running in multiple hardware setup example: P1,P2,P3,P4 or i1,i2,i3 etc.,
- The same application require to work on multiple versions of operating system ex: Win, MAC, Linux etc.;

(iv) Scalability Testing

- When the software is released, the number of users accessing the application may be limited. When the business grows, the need for more user to access the software also increased. And so more users will be given access to the Software.
- This may include increasing the no. of instance of processors of the product, data base connections etc.
- Virtually also can be tested based on the requirements for the product/application or database.

(v) Security Testing

- Securing the data and the program is very important as the data and the programs directly deals with critical details. The data abstraction must be done for different level of users.
- The right to perform certain operations must be given to only specific users.
  Each user must be uniquely, identified by UID and Password. The hackers increasing day by day, the applications must be completely shield off from unauthorized users. In the internet the security issues are equally important to the functionality of the product.
- Next level of security takes place in case of encryption of data. The data sent via wires, cables and phone lines are vulnerable to hacking. The taping of lines can not be completely prevented but if the data is scrambled in such a manner, any hackers cannot understand it. Then it is equally good enough. To achieve this, there are various measures, used for encoding and decoding messages that are transmitted. These are encryption methods being followed all over the world.

(vi) Recovery Testing

- Data is the most precious thing for the end user. The programs are mean to act on the data and based on that only business is driven.
- When an application fails (or) crashes there is always the possibilities of data being lost.
- But business depends entirely on data and the accuracy and the integrity of the data. Cannot be compromised for any reason. To test the system, whether is there any data loss due to such crashes, need to test the system to be crashed.

(vii) Usability Testing

- **The software product's prime goal is to satisfy the customer's business name.**
- Most of the people who use the software product, will be having minimize to marginal software knowledge. But will have very good business knowledge.
- Unless the software is really simple and pleasing to use, it may not get recognition from the user community.
- This usability testing involves, accessing the simplicity of product in terms of usage, pleasing sense of screens, adequacy in providing help to the users etc.

(viii) Bench Marking: (Software Comparison to others)

- When software product ready, the client will have to evaluate its performance against the product of the competitors, which serves the same functionality. This comparison is **very much essential, when the end user of many similar products & product's** features and the performance are not good, right at the first use of end user, it is difficult to get good market.
- This is normally done to both in house people and third partly agencies.

(ix) Smoke Testing

- To check the application in depth, check the basic requirements and fulfilled (or) not, suppose it is failed to reject the build and stop the testing.

Note:

WBI -> Testing efficiencies are measured in terms of no. of bugs for some line of codes. Normally the lines of code is measured KLOC (or) MLOC [Kilo (or) Million lines of code]

Software Release

- After the acceptance test is complete (including beta testing), the product is ready to be released.
- Then the program Manager from client side will give the release request.
- The SDU Project Manager, together with the test leader, and configuration liberation, prepares a list of software programs, files, database tables etc. along with their versions.
- This is called as Release Test.
- Then (i) release note → for installation information, version, bugs & solution
  (ii) Release Certificate → Details line when launched etc. are released.
- This serve as approval for releasing the software.

Requirements Traceability Matrix (RTM)
(Tracing Document)

- In this rows will have the requirements.
- For every doc [HDL, LLD] etc. there will be separate column.
- In every cell we need to state, what section in HLD addresses a particular requirement.
- In case of any missing requirement, we need to go back to document and correct it, so that it addresses the requirement.
- **The URS/SRS is the basis for the entire software product and the product's goal is to satisfy (or) address each and every one of the requirements.**
- Whenever document is prepared towards achieving this goal, the individual sections in the documents are to be verified whether they are <u>addressing the requirements</u> are not.
- Also list of requirements is often checked against the document produced, to know whether they are completely addressed (or) not.
- This is called as <u>tracing</u> requirements.
- There is a separate matrix used to know where the <u>requirements are addressed in the documents.</u> (This is called as RTM).

Requirements	HLD	LLD	Source Code	Unit Test Cases	Integration Test Cases	System Test Cases
Login						
Register etc						

- As and when the documents are produced, the author of the documents, must update the RTM, against the requirements.
- <u>Ex:</u>
  When the LLD doc- is prepared, the author must make sure, it <u>does not miss any requirements</u> and so on.
- <u>During development</u> process, RTM is used to identify whether any requirements are missed. <u>During maintenance functionality</u> also any problem occurs can be verified in RTM.

Testing and Design Requirements

- Testing is prepared on the requirements and design documents also along with the coding (programs).
- The reviews may be carried out in peer reviews (or) they may be done only by certain dedicated resources.
- During reviews, the idea is to capture any flaws in the document. These defects may be conceptual, functional, technical, editorial etc.
- The reviews are focused on the product and not on the individuals who prepared the work product.
- The SRS, HLD and LLD are reviewed for several times, to remove defects in them.
- In reviews also the defects are categorized according to their severity.

<u>Defect Analysis</u>

- When defects are found in the product, they are documented and later they are used for arriving at various <u>statistics.</u>

- The important ones are;
    (i)   Defect Distribution
    (ii)   Defect Density
    (iii) Defect Age
    (iv) Defect leakage.

- Defects are generally found in SRS review, HLD and LLD reviews, code reviews, test case review etc.
- When a particular defect is not detected and it is detected in subsequent stages the <u>rework</u> will take more time and this is called <u>defect leakage.</u>
- Defect leakage can be prevented by proper reviews at different phases in software development.
- The <u>defect age</u> is the duration between the phase when the defect is identified and rectified.
- The percentage of number of defects found out in a particular phase to total no. of defects found out in a particular phase to total no. of defects found out in the development is called <u>defect distribution.</u>
- The <u>defect density</u> is the total no. of defects per kilo lines of code (KLOC).
  (Many companies strict to factors like I bug per million lines of code).

Test Strategy Preparation (Master Test Plan)

- Before starting any testing activities, the team lead will have to think a lot and arrive at a strategy.
- This will describe the approach which has to be adopted for carrying out test activities including the planning activities.
- This is a formal document and the very first document regarding the testing area and is prepared at a very early stage in SDLC.
- The following areas are addressed in the test strategy document.

    (i)   Test Levels

    - For a particular project, what are the test levels carried out?
    - Unit, Integration and system testing will be carried out in all the projects.
    - But many times the integration (IT) and system (ST) combined. Details like this must be addressed in this section.

    (ii)   Roles and Responsibilities

    - The roles and responsibilities of test leader, individual testers, project manager, are to be clearly defined at a project level in this section.
    - In this, we have to state who reviews the test cases, test records and who approves them.
    - The documents may go through – series of reviews (or) multiple approvals, and they have to be mentioned here.
    - Testing Tools:
      Any testing tools are to be used in different test levels must be clearly identified.
      Ex: Rational test tools, selenium, QC etc.
    - This includes justifications for the tools being used in that particular test levels also.

    (iii) Risk and Mitigation
    - Any risks that will affect the testing process must be listed along with a mitigation.
    - By documenting the risks in this document, we can anticipate the occurrence of it well ahead of time and then we can proactively prevent it from occurring.

    (iv)   Regression Test Approach
    - When a problem identified the programs will be debugged and the fix will be done to the program.
    - To make sure that the fix works, the program will be tested again for the criteria.
    - Regression test will make sure that one fix does not create some other problems in that Program (or) in any other interface.

(v)   Test Groups:
- From the list of requirements we can identify related areas, whose functionality is similar. These areas are the test groups.
- [Ex: In railway system booking is in group report is another group etc.]

(vi)   Test Priorities:

- Among the test cases, we need to establish priorities. [In a two- wheeler, the engine, wheels, brakes, seat and accelerator have priority 1 towards transportation].
- In the same way test priorities (test cases levels) should be clearly mentioned in the document.
- Sometimes test priorities may be mapped to the test groups also.

(vii)   Test status collection and Reporting:

- When test cases are executed, the test lead, project manager must know, where exactly we stand in terms of testing activities.
- Also how often we collect the status is to be clearly mentioned.
- Some Companies collects status on a daily (or) weekly basis must be mentioned in document.

(viii)   Test Records Maintenance:

- When the test cases are executed was need to keep track of the execution details like
  - ✧ When it is executed?
  - ✧ Who did it?
  - ✧ How long it will work?
  - ✧ What is the result etc?
- This data must be available at a central location at all.
- This may be stored in specific directory in a Central Server and the document must say clearly about the locations and the directories.
- The naming conventions for the documents and files must also be mentioned.

(ix)   Test Summary:

- The management/stakeholders may line to have test summary on a weekly (or)   monthly basis.
- If the project is very critical, they may need it on a daily basis also.
- This section must address what kind of test summary reports will be produced for the senior management along with the frequency.
- The test strategy must give a clear vision of what the testing team will do for the whole project for the entire duration.

- This section must address what kind of test summary reports will be produced for the senior management along with.
- The test Strategy must give a clear vision of what the testing team will do for the whole project in the entire duration.
- This document will/may be presented to the client also, if needed.
- The person who prepares this document must be strong (like leader (or) best development etc) in the product domain, with good experience, as this document that is going to drive the entire team for the testing activities.
- Test Strategy must be clearly explained to the testing team at the beginning of the project.

Test Automation

Software Testing Life Cycle (STLC) - process used to test software and ensure that quality standards are met. Tests are conducted over several phases. During product development, phases of the STLC may be performed multiple times until a product is ready for release.

STLC → Software Testing Life Cycle

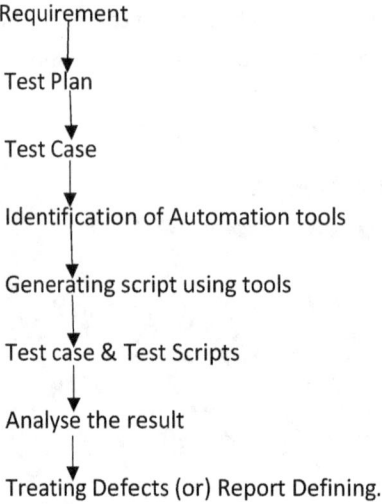

Requirement

Test Plan

Test Case

Identification of Automation tools

Generating script using tools

Test case & Test Scripts

Analyse the result

Treating Defects (or) Report Defining.

Automated testing - The application of software tools to automate a manual process of reviewing & validating a software product. Modern agile & DevOps software projects now include automated testing from inception stage.

Some Automation Testing Tools Example

1. Katalon

The Katalon Platform is a low-code and scalable automation testing tool for web, API, desktop (Windows), and mobile applications.

2. Selenium

Selenium is an open-source tool that automates web browsers.

3. Appium

Like Selenium, Appium is also an open-source automation testing tool, but for mobile applications.

4. TestComplete

TestComplete can automate functional UI testing for desktop, mobile, and web applications.

5. CyPress

Purely supporting JavaScript frameworks, Cypress is a developer-centric automation tool for end-to-end web testing.

6. Postman

Postman is one of the most widely used automation testing tools for API.

Sample Testing tools for Automation

Postman

- Postman is a scalable API testing tool that integrates into CI/CD pipeline.
- Simplifies API workflow in testing and development.
- API allows software applications to communicate with each other via API calls.
- ✓ Accessibility – Just need to log-in to own accounts making it easy to access files anytime, anywhere if Postman application is installed in the system (with browser).
- ✓ Use of Collections – Allows users create collections for their Postman API calls. Each collection can create sub folders & multiple requests. This helps in organizing test suites.
- ✓ Collaboration – Collections & environments can be imported/exported making it easy to share files. Direct link can also be used to share collections.
- ✓ Creating Environments – Multiple environments aids in less repetition of tests as one can use the same collection but for a different environment. The parameterization will take place in this context.
- ✓ Tests Creation – Test checkpoints to verify for successful HTTP response status can be added to each Postman API calls which help ensure test coverage.
- ✓ Automation Testing – Through the use of the Collection Runner /Newman, tests can run in multiple iterations saving time for repetitive tests.
- ✓ Debugging – Postman console helps to check what data has been retrieved making it easy to debug tests.
- ✓ Continuous Integration – It supports continuous integration, development practices are maintained.

Selenium

Selenium is an open-source tool that automates web browsers. It provides a single interface that allows to write test scripts in programming languages like Ruby, Java, NodeJS, PHP, Perl, Python, and C#, etc.

- Supported browsers: Chrome, Firefox, IE, Microsoft Edge, Opera, Safari, etc.
- Testing on local or remote machines via the Selenium server.
- Parallel and cross-browser executions to reduce execution time and increase test coverage.
- Integrations with other testing frameworks (e.g., TestNG for reporting) and CI/CD tools.

Types of Automated Testing (Examples)

- ➢ Functional Testing
- ➢ Unit Testing
- ➢ Integration Testing
- ➢ Smoke Testing
- ➢ Non-functional Testing
- ➢ Performance Testing
- ➢ Regression Testing

Agile Testing

Software testing practice that follows the Agile development methodology. Projects tend to evolve during each sprint among all. Agile testing focuses on ensuring quality in all the Agile software development process.

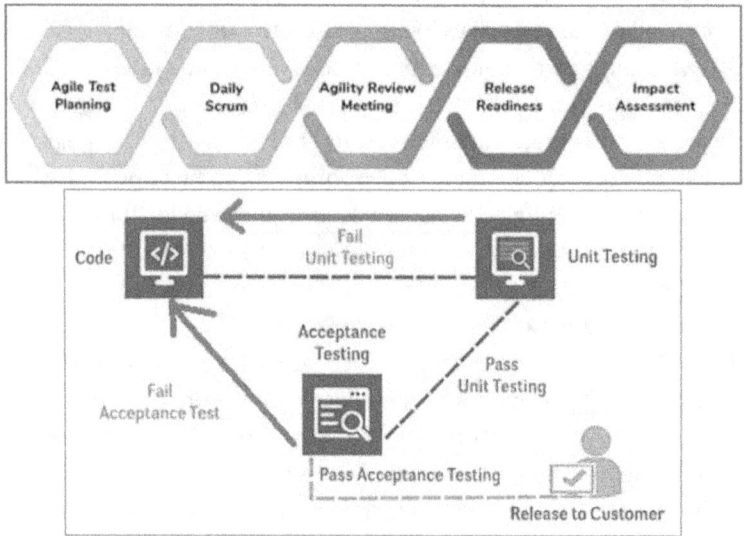

DevOps Testing

DevOps Testing is the process of automating and smoothing out the entire delivery life cycle of software. A lot of companies employ DevOps testing strategies by starting with the agile practice of Continuous Integration (CI). Overall DevOps lifecyce stages shown below.

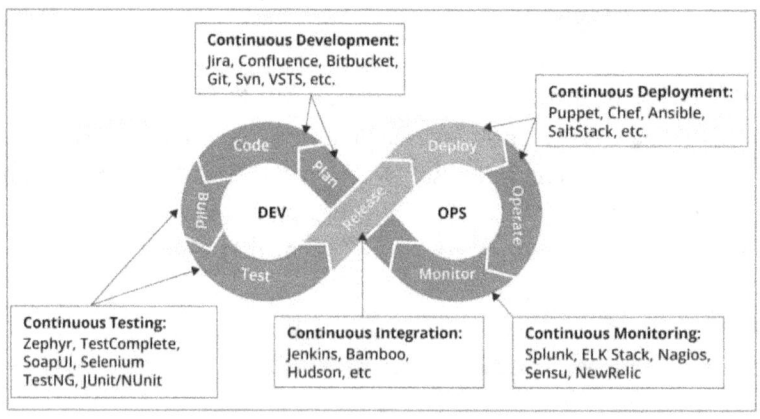

Test Management Tool

There are applications like JIRA/Taiga/QAComplete/TestPad etc very useful to track and maintain the whole testing process from the inception to post-live check or maintenance.

TAIGA (Open Source)

JIRA

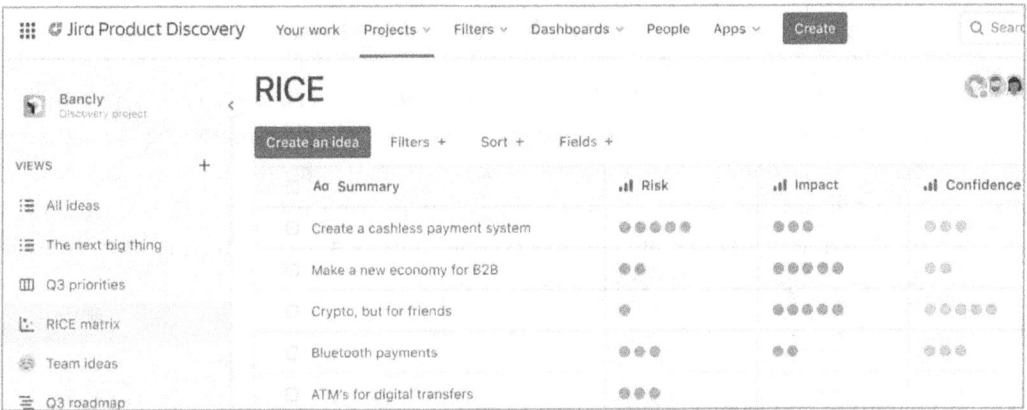

IBM Rational Quality Manager

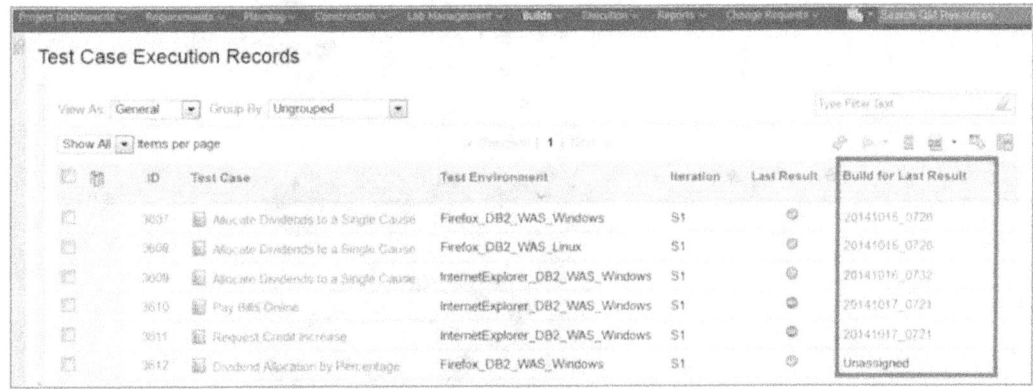

Summary & Conclusion

➤ This document covers mostly basics of testing (both manual and automated) types with few examples.

➤ People can make use of this material to understand what are the necessary steps and documents required in any testing environment.

➤ SDLC and STLC are covered in brief to understand the flow.

➤ Test plan preparation covered at high level to assist how to make the plan effectively.

➤ People also will understand how to write test cases as per the requirements given & RTM.

➤ Special testing methods are important depending on the types of testing used.

➤ Defects, debugging and testing details to know the difference and understand clearly.

➤ Few examples of automated testing and tools covered importantly.

➤ Agile and DevOps flow and testing with test management tools included.

➤ More details to be covered in the next version/release.

In "Manual and Automated Software Testing," we aim to equip you with the knowledge, tools, and techniques necessary to excel in the world of software testing. Whether you are a beginner seeking to understand the basics or an experienced professional looking to broaden your skill set, this book provides a simple guide to ensure software quality. Join us on this exciting journey as we unravel the complexities of software testing and empower you to deliver exceptional software products.

Thank You